Illustrators at work

Illustrators at work

ROBIN JACQUES

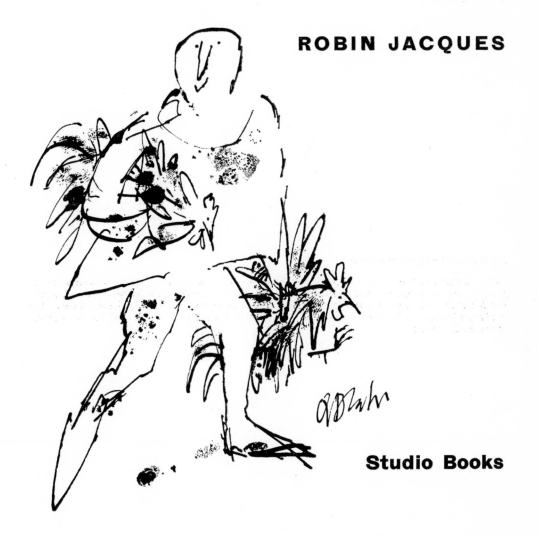

Studio Books

To Azetta

Acknowledgements

I wish to thank all the artists and publishers who were kind enough to lend me drawings and to grant me rights of reproduction. Valuable help and advice were given me by Miss Diana Klemin and Mr Pyke Johnson of Doubleday Inc, for which I am most grateful. My thanks are also due to Mr Huddleston of W. Heinemann Ltd, Mrs Ashton, Librarian of *Punch*, and Mr Peter Harle of the *Radio Times*.

PUBLISHED BY STUDIO BOOKS (LONGACRE PRESS LTD)
161 FLEET STREET · LONDON · EC4
PRINTED IN GREAT BRITAIN BY STAPLES PRINTERS LTD, ROCHESTER

Contents

Introduction

Illustrators set about their work in many different ways. The professional black-and-white illustrators with whom this book is concerned are highly individual performers in a very competitive field and, like actors, are required to undertake engagements on a number of different levels. Books, magazines, advertising and more recently television, are some of the media in which they are invited to work. To operate efficiently in these varied departments they have adopted their own, sometimes highly idiosyncratic methods of work and it is with these that this short book is largely concerned. It occurred to me that an account of the illustrator at work might be of interest, not only to the illustration student and those engaged in his future employment in one form or another, but to those who enjoy graphic work of quality.

As a framework to this general aim, I have included a chapter on some of the early artists whose work forms the basis of the English illustration tradition, and this is followed by a short account of the means by which the artist's work is printed and some general information about the preparation of black-and-white drawings for reproduction. Later, after the main section which is devoted to the work of the artists themselves, I have added a series of short notes for the student.

My choice of contemporary artists for inclusion in the book was conditioned by several factors. In the first place, I hoped to display the work of as varied a group as I could muster. I wanted advertising and television illustrators as well as book and magazine artists, though these are not necessarily mutually exclusive pursuits. Again, several excellent artists were excluded since their talents seemed to me more directly decorative than illustrative. Finally, a very small number of artists failed to respond to my request for specimens of work.

6

1 · The illustrative tradition

a note on some of the great illustrators of the past

A number of scholarly books have been written on the history of illustration and they make absorbing reading. Nor is the subject entirely a narrowly restricted one, of interest only to a few dim pedants in some dull academic backwater. Few of us, as children, were not exposed to the magic of at least some of the Victorian masters, Tenniel, Greenaway, Cruikshank and Doré. Out of our early responses to these nursery loves grew an abiding affection which is shared by many people to whom books, as entertainment, may now mean little or nothing.

Although this book is not intended as an historical study, I believe that it will soon be seen how many of our contemporary black-and-white artists are working in some variant of the main English illustrative tradition and, even where there are few evidences of traditional influences to be found in their work, many illustrators will admit to a passion for one or another of the founding fathers.

In these first pages you will find examples of the work of some of the great Victorians and even earlier artists, all of whom have had some hand in giving the illustrated book in this country its particular flavour. Nor were these artists always book-illustrators. The searching drawings of some of the greatest European painters, such as Rembrandt and Goya, have swayed a number of our illustrators toward working more directly from life, eschewing a general reliance on memory and reference material. What is gained, they claim, is a greater freshness and sense of immediacy so that the drawing is not contrived from a jobber's stock of all-purpose clichés.

At the same time, the subjective and inward-looking romanticism of the English imagination still exerts a powerful magnetic pull in the opposite direction. William Blake, Samuel Palmer and, to some extent, the Pre-Raphaelite Brotherhood, were the

Etching by Goya, from *Disasters of the War*

archetypes of what might be called the 'literary' tradition in illustration, while Rowlandson, Gillray, Cruikshank and Doré could loosely be considered as forming its 'gothic' extremity.

Graphic talent in Britain, however, is, and has always been, too abundant and the executants too varied to allow rigid categorization. Apart from the natural process of stylistic cross-semination, from time to time technical developments have opened up new opportunities and to these our artists have not been slow to respond. In 1890, when the *Daily Graphic* introduced itself as the first daily illustrated newspaper, it carried the work of a gifted group of artists, the first to draw expressly for the new method of direct mechanical reproduction, as opposed to the existing 'interpretive' wood-block process.

Wood-engravings by Thomas Bewick

Among the most revered of the early English illustrators is Thomas Bewick, whose wood engravings are little miracles of ordered observation, encapsulating a hungry intellectual search for the unsentimental truth about country life. I believe Bewick to be central to the best in the English graphic tradition. His was the analytical method of George Stubbs, that most English of English painters, who wrung the neck of Nature until it rendered up its essential truth. Bewick knew, as I believe no man since has known, how to organize from a few inches of wood block a timeless comment on the relation of man to nature. And it was an unmistakably English comment, its flavour that of his native Northumbria, forthright, independant and impatient of fashionable 'chi-chi'. The technique of wood engraving, which has not changed in any important respect from Bewick's day, is briefly described in the next chapter.

George Cruikshank:
Monmouth Street, Soho

The novels of Dickens were well served by a number of gifted artists. It was, however, the peculiar quirky genius of George Cruikshank that became most closely identified with the novelist's work. In the course of his long life he illustrated many classics and those seem to me most successful in which free rein could be given to his marked gifts for portraying the grotesque and sardonic aspects of life. Like the earlier artists, Rowlandson and Gillray, his was the robust irreverence of the pre-Victorian spirit, and the sentimental scenes of domestic felicity, so dear to a later public, were utterly alien to him.

Gustave Doré, whose formidable talents brought him an international reputation, illustrated very many books. Born in France in 1828, his professional career began at 16, when he joined the staff of the *Journal Pour Rire*. Before he died, at the age of 51, he had illustrated the Bible, Balzac's *Contes Drolatiques*, *Don Quixote*, Dante's *Inferno*, *Paradise Lost*, the works of Rabelais, the *Fables* of La Fontaine and many other books. The French romantic exuberance of the 1840s is reflected in all of Doré's work and, if his enormous output was not uniformly excellent, given the right subject he could do wonders. His powers of organization and his sheer energy were almost always present, and he responded with such vitality to the challenge of his subject that a convincing case could be made out for him as the greatest of all illustrators. In his short life, he also found time to execute many large historical and religious paintings but these seem to us now no more distinguished than the enormous acreage of subject pictures turned out by his academic contemporaries. No, it was as an illustrator that he seems giant size, his industry and imagination positively Balzacian.

Gustav Doré, from Balzac's *Droll Tales*

Sir John Tenniel, from *Alice's Adventures in Wonderland*

A comparison of the raw humour of Cruikshank or the explosive talents of Doré with the classic suavity of Sir John Tenniel is a reflection in microcosm of the general drift of Victorian taste. Tenniel's work, like that of his friend, John Leech, has much of the *gravitas* beloved of the Victorians and a new dignity very different from the unbuttoned high spirits of the earlier graphic artists. When he died in 1914 at the age of 94, Tenniel, who had worked for *Punch* for more than fifty years, had seen its aggressively radical beginnings grow into a blimpish philistinism. He illustrated more than twenty books, the best known of which are *Lalla Rookh* and the two Lewis Carroll classics, *Alice's Adventures in Wonderland* and *Through the Looking Glass*. The Alice series of drawings are particularly effective since the matter-of-factness of his

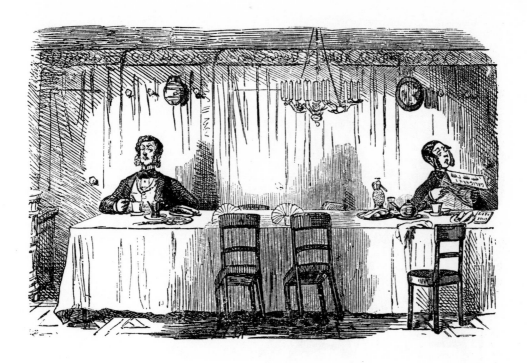

John Leech, 'The Briton abroad' (Reproduced by permission of *Punch*)

style exactly complements Carroll's inspired surrealism.

Tenniel's contemporary, John Leech, also drew for *Punch*. In his early work, his indebtedness to Cruikshank is clear to see, and his drawings of the London poor in 1841 have the authentic Dickensian pathos. His temperament and background, however, equipped him singularly well to chronicle the bucolic tastes of the Victorian landed gentry and his sporting scenes have the genuine robustness of the country life of the period.

Leech became, in his short working life, the link between the unsentimental sharp-shooting of Rowlandson, Gillray and Cruikshank and the more ponderous tastes of the later Victorian artists.

Charles Keene, drawing engraved by John Swain
(Reproduced by permission of *Punch*)

To some extent the Pre-Raphaelite Brotherhood represents the aesthetic counter-blast to orthodox mid-Victorian values, and the movement threw up some formidable graphic talents. Few of them were concerned with the day-to-day professionalism of the magazine and book illustration of the period, but Ford Madox Brown and John Millais were draughtsmen of considerable powers.

Possibly of all the black-and-white artists of his period Charles Keene (1823–91) has been most admired. Whistler thought him the greatest English artist since Hogarth; Sickert exhorted his students to look ever more closely at his work, and today's illustrators are almost unanimous in their acclaim. Keene was a superb draughtsman, though perhaps not so impressive an illustrator. The books for which he made drawings are few, and he may well have found himself better suited by the freedom for anecdotal comment available to him in the pages of *Punch*. His drawings are the least contrived in the world and they have an enforced grace that is quite unmistakable.

George du Maurier, 'A tragedy on the Great Northern'. (Reproduced by permission of *Punch*)

George du Maurier made his debut in the 'sixties and was thereafter fully employed by the magazines of the day, *Once a Week*, *Punch*, *London Society* and a number of others. Today he is remembered primarily as a satirist and student of the social scene of his time, and his work in this genre is indeed highly accomplished. He was also the author of three novels, one of which, *Trilby*, was an enormous popular success and is still widely read today. For my part, I have always preferred the subtly composed and deeply moving drawings that he made for *Once a Week* during the 'sixties to the charming ephemera of his later work. One of these drawings is shown below.

Aubrey Beardsley,
'The Wagnerians'

Fin-de-siècle England abounded in magazines of widely varied literary and political tendencies. Among them, the short-lived *Yellow Book* became the erstwhile club with which the aesthetic *avant-garde* laid about the bourgeoisie. Its principal standard-bearers, indeed its co-editors, were the poet Arthur Symons and Aubrey Beardsley, whose extraordinary drawings shocked and incensed the general public who read into them implications of 'unspeakable depravity', which Beardsley was more than happy to do nothing to dispel. Cooler eyes have since reappraised him. The *frisson* of shock is no longer felt and we are left with an artist of real but limited originality, an excellent technician who might, had he lived beyond his 26 years, have developed very differently.

Another contributor to the *Yellow Book*, and one whose work is far more to contemporary taste, was A. S. Hartrick, nearer in spirit to Keene and Sickert than to the 'literary' illustrators of the 'high decadence'. His sober, unemphatic drawings are a delight to those who now feel that the painterly virtues are or should be supreme in the practice of illustration.

Considerably nearer in time to us was Arthur Rackham (1867–1939), who, unlike most of the other artists so far considered, was exclusively a book illustrator. His imaginative powers, sure draughtsmanship and subtly muted colours were very much

16

A. S. Hartrick, drawing of Joseph Pennell

in demand, and he responded best to fantastic and horrific subject matter. His essential gentleness of spirit, however, always conditioned his imagination, and his ghouls and hobgoblins seem secretly benevolent.

These, then, were some of the artists who went before and laid down the great tradition of English black-and-white. There were, of course, many others whose work will be found copiously dealt with elsewhere, but in this brief survey I have chosen only those who seem to me relevant to subsequent developments in the medium. The work of all these artists, with the exception of Beardsley, Rackham and Bewick, who made his own engravings, was usually cut directly on wood-blocks by commercial engravers, considerable craftsmen themselves. These men, who sometimes worked as a group on a single large drawing, each taking a detached section of wood-block, were able by their great skill and experience, to interpret the variety of graphic styles employed by the illustrators. In the next chapter, the technique of wood-engraving and the tools employed are briefly examined.

Drawing by Richard Sickert

2 · Processes of reproduction

a description of the methods of graphic reproduction as they affect the work of the black-and-white artist

In this book, the whole range of the reproductive processes cannot properly be covered and I shall restrict myself to describing very simply those in general use for black-and-white work. The artists themselves will have more to say about their own handling of their respective mediums.

It seems proper to begin with the earliest and most direct methods of graphic reproduction, commonly called autographic.

Woodcuts and linocuts

Here the artist first draws his design on the block, either wood or lino, gouges out with a knife the parts which are not to print and is so left with isolated areas in relief. This is his printing surface. This surface is then inked and an impression taken off on paper by means of a hand-press. In general, however, the woodcut and linocut are more commonly employed for colour work with which we are not here concerned.

Wood-engraving

Happily, there is still a good deal of book-illustration carried out by the wood-engraver although, to the purist, his art is no longer genuinely autographic in that his original engraving has often to be duplicated by the electro plate for extensive printings. The wood-engraver's block is usually of boxwood, which offers a hard even surface which will take the finest, most delicately cut incisions. Long ago, I was given a set of engraver's tools and, with the help of a more experienced friend, took my first tentative steps. I soon found it to be a medium of curious complexity and, try as I might, I could not get my design 'off the ground'. I studied at length the work of the current

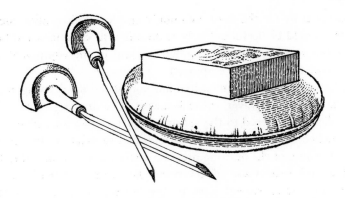

Some tools of the wood-engraver

masters of the art, but had finally to admit defeat. I remember, too, how reluctantly I parted with the tools, which were delicately beautiful, having each the 'right' shape and fitness for use. There was first the little sandbag, covered in leather, on which the wood-block rested four-square. The surface of the block I had painted black and on this I had made a careful drawing in white pencil. Along the edges of my white lines I gouged and cut away, leaving them in relief and bringing into use the four bull-stickers and scorpers that lay by my drawing hand. These needed constant sharpening to retain their clear cutting points. When I thought my engraving finished I took off an impression on a small hand-press.

Lithography

The uses of lithography are now so widespread and so varied that it might be best to begin by establishing its basic principle. The word lithography derives from the Greek 'litho' which means stone. Lithography then, by definition, is the art of drawing on stone. In the course of time, however, other materials such as aluminium and zinc plates and, more recently, treated plastic sheets have been employed.

In principle, the drawing is carried out with a greasy substance, crayon or ink. Then, since grease and water are mutually repellant, by moistening the surface with water the undrawn areas are 'stopped out', i.e. the ink adheres to the stone or metal only where it has been covered by the drawing so that a reversed but facsimile print may be taken from it. The drawing is carried out in brush, chalk or pen and a satisfying variety of textures can be produced in a single drawing. Owing to the unwieldy nature of the stone, it has become more general to make one's design on paper which is then transferred to the stone or lithographic plate.

The photographic processes

The line-block

The line-drawing is by far the most commonly employed illustration method today, and I feel that it would be useful not only to describe the capacities and limitations of the line-block but to add a rather extended account of the equipment used by the artist and the ways in which it is employed.

First then, let us suppose that the artist has completed his drawing and that it has been sent to the process-engraver or block-maker. The drawing is photographed and the negative image transferred to the sensitized surface of a zinc plate. This is then mechanically etched so that only the areas intended to print are left in relief on the plate. The tonal values of the drawing must be arrived at by means other than washes or watered-down ink since these effects cannot be accommodated by the line-block. On the other hand, given careful work by the block-maker, the most delicate line-drawing will reproduce so long as really black ink is used, and so long as the paper surface on which it is to be printed is suitably receptive. In recent years, the Dow Etch Process of block-making has enormously improved the sharpness of the line-block and renders the printed image really faithfully. Again, where a drawing contains unusually delicate passages of drawing it is customary to employ what is called a fine-line block, which is more expensive but better able to deal with such detail than is the ordinary line-block.

A comparison of a drawing reproduced the same size as the original, and the same drawing considerably reduced in scale

From the cover of *A Fearful Joy*, by Joyce Cary
By courtesy of Doubleday & Co Inc, New York

The half-tone block

The second main photographic process employed for the reproduction of black-and-white drawings is the half-tone block. This is more generally used to deal with the subtle tonal graduations found in photography and wash-drawings, with which the line-block is not equipped to deal. In essence, one arrives at a half-tone block by passing a fine grid-screen between the photo-lens and the sensitized photographic plate, so that the negative receives an image made up of an ordered area of dots of different sizes. In positive, these dots resolve themselves into a very fair approximation of the tonal values of the original. Other variants on the wash drawing may be dealt with by a number of different technical formulae such as the combination line and half-tone block and the deep-etched half-tone block. Rarely successful in black-and-white book illustration, the half-tone block is in much more general use in newspapers and magazines to reproduce fashion drawings, short story illustrations and press advertisements.

Photogravure

The black-and-white artist will find his work reproduced from time to time by the photogravure process which, although superficially similar to half-tone, is technically quite different. The infinitely fine dotted screen that can be seen to break up the image is arrived at in a completely different way. Where, in the half-tone block the tiny dots are printed from the raised or relief surface of the block, the gravure dots are etched into a copper cylinder so that the tiny cavities lie *beneath* the surface of the plate itself. The main disadvantage of the process from the artist's point of view is that an overall tonal levelling out seems inescapable. His full blacks seem rarely as dense as in his original and the high-lighted white areas tend to lack crisp definition.

The process whereby the design to be printed lies below the printing surface, as in photogravure, is called intaglio, as opposed to relief, printing or planographic printing, *e.g.*, lithography and collotype. Other intaglio methods include line-etching, dry point, copper and steel engraving and aquatint. All of these have been used in the past for the illustration of books but are rarely employed today.

3 · Line-drawing for reproduction

the author's general procedure for planning and carrying out a black-and-white illustration

The illustrator's equipment

In the course of time, by trial and error, the artist will have arrived at his own chosen *modus operandi*. He will have found the paper most suitable for his particular drawing method, and his pens, inks and other materials will be those best able to bring about the effects he seeks.

Although, as will be seen by the comments of the artists in a later chapter, their methods of work vary considerably, it may be useful to describe what general equipment seems to me an absolute necessity. First of all, a desk big enough to accommodate the largest drawing the artist is likely to be called on to make. Its size will also to some extent be conditioned by the scale to which he normally works. He may, for instance, draw two or three times larger than reproduction size, in which case he will need ample room to spread himself. He may be, by nature, an untidy worker, in which case he is best advised to allow room enough to accommodate the pyramid of reference material, correspondence, final demands, cheque stubs, etc., which will surely accumulate. The man with too restricted a working area is hopelessly hamstrung. The drawing papers on which he works are best kept in a drawer and free from dirt. His inks, pencils, brushes, rubbers and pens will be close to hand. He will also have by him a pot or tube of process white with which he can correct awkward or ill-considered passages of drawing. He will probably also have a sharp-bladed knife or scalpel with a fine enough point to scratch out ink blots or, if necessary, cut out patches of infelicitous drawing. And if, before cutting, he slips another sheet of the same paper under his drawing and presses sufficiently hard to cut through both sheets he will be able to patch in with Scotch tape the second section of paper on which to make his revisions.

The purely mechanical aids he will need will probably include a large and a small set square, a typographical ruler and a basic set of drawing instruments. He should also have a desk light bright enough to work by, late into the night if necessary. In passing, I have found it wise to place a fairly large sheet of dullish coloured paper beneath the drawing in order to diminish the reflected glare from the desk light over long periods of work.

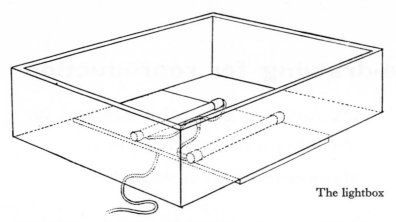

I should like to add to this basic list one or two refinements which may prove useful. The first of these is a lightbox. With this one can trace through on to drawing paper a sketch placed underneath. The sketch will probably be the last of a series made on layout or tracing paper and which represent the developing phases of the illustration. Once the sketch is traced through in pencil, one is ready to go to work on the final drawing. The lightbox is simply constructed by making a wooden framework open top and bottom, as shown in the drawing. Over the top, a piece of stout glass is fitted or slotted and across the open bottom a section of wood is nailed, to which can be attached one or two strip lights. These will throw up through the glass enough light to pass through both sheets of paper and so make the tracing easy.

I also like to have by me a packet of paper tissues for which I have found many uses. To prevent my pencils and pens from rolling about or falling to the floor, I have them laid out on a strip of corrugated paper tacked to the table. On this they rest in an orderly rank and are quickly found.

To work

The black-and-white artist is a curious amalgam of a number of things. He must be, in part, journalist, ideas-man, entertainer and commentator. But above all else he is a draughtsman and, without full command of his means of expression, his excellence in any other department of his trade is rendered worthless.

The following notes are intended for the aspirant illustrator. I shall assume that, by dint of hard work, good advice, and a clear-eyed assessment of his talents, the student has satisfied himself that he wishes to be a black-and-white illustrator and not some other sort of graphic practitioner for whom proficiency in line-drawing may be relatively unimportant. For line-drawing is the bed-rock on which black-and-white illustration is built, although, in the course of time, the artist will certainly be called on to perform in other mediums, too.

Materials

A commissioned illustration that cannot be reproduced by the methods available to the publisher will almost certainly never see the light of day. It may be a drawing of infinite sensitivity, but it will have failed as an illustration since its appropriate context has been denied it. Thus the artist is forcibly reminded that his drawing must always be made in such a way that its effects will permit of faithful reproduction, in our present case, by the line-block. While it is true that almost all line-drawings can now be reasonably well reproduced by one or other of the photographic processes, it is not always the case that the publisher is prepared to face the necessary additional cost. You may, for instance, have carried out your illustration in pencil with delicately modelled tonal areas, an approach that seems to you entirely appropriate to the text involved. Such a drawing, it's true, has proved most effective on a number of occasions but it will certainly have had to be reproduced by a process other than the line-block. By referring back to the short description of a line-block on page 20, you will see that, by its very nature, it cannot adequately cope with pencil drawing. Remember, too, that even when you draw boldly in brush or pen, your ink must be a full true black, undiluted and free-flowing. The illustrator will quickly discover for himself which of the available commercial inks best suits his purpose and, if he's wise, he will be ready to jettison the bottle the moment he finds his pen clogging with the matted residue at the bottom. It is a poor economy to waste time digging gouts of coagulated ink off nibs or brushes.

Any discussion of the tools of the illustrator's trade must certainly include the papers or boards on which he works. Very probably he will choose to have by him a variety of drawing surfaces since, if he is versatile, and he must certainly try to be, he will be asked to make drawings for a number of different purposes. Naturally, these purposes will, very largely, condition the character of the drawing which will in turn affect the paper used. At the same time, the artist will probably find that he comes to rely, more and more, on one paper surface, almost certainly because this has not only proved most responsive to his style of drawing but is versatile enough to allow him to carry out work of many different types on it. In this connection, I myself have found a hard-surfaced near-transparent paper which, for my purposes, combines the virtues of a number of other excellent papers. Its surface is non-porous but with just enough 'bite' to provide the degree of resistance that I like to feel against the nib. It is, moreover, of a consistent whiteness and is so nearly transparent that one's final sketch drawing can be very simply traced through on the lightbox. This particular paper happens to suit *me* very well but would certainly not measure up to the requirements of other artists who, because of their different styles, need other qualities in their papers and boards. Similarly, his choice of pens and brushes will directly reflect the illustrator's personal method, and although he may have by him the full range of available brushes and nibs, he may finally come to rely on very few of these to carry out his work.

The commission

We have reached the point where, having examined the illustrator's equipment and with some knowledge of the mechanical limitations imposed on him by the line-block, we are ready to watch him undertake a hypothetical commission. Let us suppose that the artist has been asked to make a small black-and-white illustration for the jacket of a paper-back edition of a well-known classic, possibly *Wuthering Heights*. The drawing will be required to fill a pre-ordained space in a systematized design format, so that the artist already knows what other material will appear on the jacket and what its position will be in relation to his drawing. Thus he is left with an area approximately $3\frac{1}{4} \times 2\frac{1}{2}$ in. within which to carry out his drawing. Our hypothetical jacket then, might look something like the diagram, top left, on page 27, with the dotted outline in the centre representing the area available for illustration.

Reading the book

If the book is new to him (and even if it isn't) the artist must come by a copy and carefully read or re-read the narrative. His reading will be, at one and the same time, an attempt to feel his way to the very essence of the book and a search for some central image that will convey its general flavour. Now this period of imaginative gestation can prove a strange and rather nerving experience, a phase during which the artist's illustrative sense may be pulled inconclusively this way and that. It may be, for example, that his cast of mind and the nature of his personal talent predispose him to take on an aspect of the story that he knows is really only marginal to the heart of the matter. So here, even before putting pencil to paper, he may be in difficulties and obliged to re-think his approach. In fact, his only recourse is to return to the narrative. Somewhere there he must find his answer. He may find himself reluctantly forced to eschew his first choice for illustration, a subject that he knows will allow him to display his skill to advantage, for another that more truthfully reflects the real marrow of the book itself.

The rough stage

The illustrator may have been asked to submit a rough version of his subject to the publisher before moving on to his final drawing. Few artists really like to do this since they fear that, once the publisher has approved a rough, no further development of the drawing is permissible. But the publisher too has his point of view. It was he, after all, who commissioned the drawing and, in the case of our imaginary book jacket, the drawing forms the most important part of the 'package' whose contents he hopes to sell. Naturally, he will want to satisfy himself that the drawing will not be simply an idiosyncratic piece of self-indulgence on the artist's part, but the attractive and persuasive focal point of the jacket.

Our rough for *Wuthering Heights* could, I think, quite reasonably be carried out in pencil. No colour is involved and a crisp sketch can be made quite adequately to indicate accented areas of light and shade, so that the publisher has before him a fair approximation of the final drawing. The composition, once the subject has been decided on, will be conditioned by the shape of the space available to the artist. Indeed, the shape itself may directly sway his choice of subject, and here too he may be obliged to jettison his first idea in favour of another that falls more snugly into

Wuthering Heights

Emily Bronte

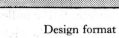
Design format

Artist's pencil rough

Finished drawing,
(by courtesy of Doubleday
& Co Inc, New York)

place in his allotted area.

It sometimes happens that the publisher asks the artist to put up more than one rough for consideration. On the whole, I feel that this is not a really helpful move since, once the artist has found the 'image' that he feels he can do most to dramatize, the intensity of his attack on it may well be diminished by a series of stabs at other subjects within the book. Naturally, a complete set of illustrations for the book is another exercise entirely and one to which the artist would have to respond quite differently.

Our illustrator, then, has brought all his skill to bear on producing his sketch. If he is wise, he will have carried it out to the scale to which he intends to make his final drawing. The publisher will be practised enough to visualize its ultimate effect in its printed size. I myself tend to draw only a very little 'up' on reproduction size, although it is more generally the case that line-drawings for reproduction are made considerably larger in scale than this.

The final drawing — stage 1

When the rough, duly approved by the publisher, is back in the hands of the artist he is all but ready to go to work on his final drawing. There are, however, one or two preliminaries. My own procedure at this stage is first to re-read the relevant passage in the narrative to make absolutely sure that no visual gaffe has slipped into the drawing, unnoticed by either the publisher or me and exposing us later to the raillery of some sharp-eyed reader, who may have noticed that I have endowed the clean-shaven with moustaches or substituted an Ulster for a Burberry or any of a hundred other things. Such pedants abound and form a tiny but irritating part of the illustrator's burden, unloved and unlovely but not to be gainsaid!

This is the moment too for clarifying details indicated only summarily in the sketch. The rigging of a ship or the leathers of a horse, correct period furniture and aspects of season and climate as they may affect lighting, landscape and interiors, must all be taken into account. In general, it behoves the illustrator to cover as much of this ground as possible at the rough stage. As he grows more experienced he will find he has absorbed, by dint of necessity, a mass of incidental data of this type which he will have trained himself to bring to bear at will. Then again, he will need an extensive collection of research and reference books as well as access to the best library in his district. Many illustrators are industrious enough always to carry a sketchbook in which to jot down details of interest which may have no immediate use but on which they can call later. Everybody goes about his research differently but go about it he certainly must, no matter how ephemeral the nature of his commission.

My own way with the modifications which may be necessary is to lay a sheet of tracing paper over my rough and carefully re-draw in detail what needs to be clarified. At the same time, I may change the composition slightly, possibly pointing up the action or eliminating some fussy irrelevancy. My object will be to give a final balance and tautness to the elements of the drawing, in preparation for the finished work.

The final drawing — stage 2

I now have before me, apart from the rough, a detailed pencil drawing on tracing paper, which forms the linear framework on which my final drawing will be based and which lacks only tonal modelling. This finalized rough I place on the lightbox and carefully trace through on to drawing paper, lightly indicating in pencil shading the tonal accents used in the publisher's rough. Here at last is my final base drawing and I am ready to press on to my work in pen and ink.

I have always found it wisest, at this stage, first to establish 'identities' since, if one runs into difficulties later, it may be extremely difficult to save the drawing from a deal of patching and scratching. A book's characters do, after all, tend to outweigh its other considerations, and if they fail to convince the illustration is doing its job poorly. Once the faces and identifying factors are firmly drawn in ink, I feel free to build up the rest of the composition. It happens that, in my rough and final drawings for *Wuthering Heights*, shown in the text, I have so composed the design that full faces are not seen. Cathy's distant figure and the half-profiled Heathcliffe must then be drawn in such a way that their separate natures are implied. I have tried to do this, first by angling the tormented Heathcliffe spikily against the sky and siting him so that he seems to grow like a monolith out of the rock. In Cathy's case, she forms a tiny windswept figure at the centre of a stormy landscape, presaging her turbulent elemental spirit. This effect is accented by a swirling back-drop of storm-clouds.

Now my drawing is finished. Here and there, I have had to apply process white to areas where I may have thrown a blot or where my pen line may have coarsened. Possibly I may have wanted to cut out a figure more crisply from its tonal background by partly edging it with white. We have gone step by step through the stages of preparing for reproduction a line illustration of a very straightforward type. We might have chosen for exposition any one of a dozen or more different illustrative problems but, in essence, I feel we have taken a basic situation common to them all. By this I mean that we have considered how to put together a black-and-white illustration for a set subject, we have pondered briefly the question of what to draw and why, the submission of the rough, the research and reference material and finally the execution of the finished drawing. But what we have covered is still only the general illustration method of one artist. Later we shall see how varied are the mental and technical approaches of other illustrators.

Before moving on to a survey of individual work by illustrators I should like to give two examples of the sort of problem that, unless squarely faced, tends to inhibit the student's development. Both of them really involve questions of taste, and for this reason each artist must apply his own criteria to their solution. Each is so intimately bound up with everyday questions of technique that I believe the proper place to discuss them is within the general context of methods of work.

Internal scale — compositional proportion

The difficulty of arriving at a suitable scale *within* the drawing is one that taxes many students. Should the action or centre of interest be sited in the near-middle distance or cinematically inflated into a close-up? And is there something intrinsically tasteless and vulgar, as is sometimes implied, in the latter approach? The answer to the last question is, I am sure, a firm 'No', since the artistic validity of the close-up in illustration has been demonstrated over and over again. On the other hand, what is equally certain is that it should be handled with discretion, since its dramatic effect may often be too emphatic for its literary context. My own view is that every drawing should, as far as is possible, complement its textual setting. No rules exist as to what is or is not 'done' in illustration. The artist must feel free to compose his drawing as he 'feels' it and, with growing experience, he will find that the internal problems of scale and proportion come to resolve themselves. At the same time he must be wary. He must be quick to eschew an over-reliance on one compositional formula since this may rapidly become a cliché.

The use of photography

There is no doubt that photography can be a real and vital source of illustrative ideas, providing a wonderful documentary record of events and period atmosphere. A careful study of genre photography, where it is available, can often do more to shape an illustrator's handling of a subject than long hours spent poring over fashion prints and contemporary engravings. A fresh illustrative approach may perhaps be suggested by the shape of a skirt in motion or the tilt of a billycock in some dim Victorian photograph. Painters, too, have responded with enthusiasm to the possibilities of photography. Artists as different as Delacroix, Degas, Sickert and Bacon have all turned it to account and, more recently, the Anglo-American 'pop-art' movement has made great play with its everyday applications. Certainly, photography has proved of enormous value to artists and illustrators and is likely to continue to do so.

The negative aspect of its uses in illustration, however, is all too abundantly evident. The cheaper women's magazines and tawdrier paperback jackets rely almost entirely on artfully composed illustrations unashamedly copied from a photo original. These sad hybrids lack both the documentary interest of good photography and the genuinely original flavour of a true illustration.

The lesson, I believe, is clear for all to see. Photography, like any other heaven sent blessing, must be used with discrimination and not abused. Its capacity to evoke for the artist the true mood of a not too distant period is part of his armoury, as is its everyday use as a record of technical detail that may not be available in any other form. But he should firmly resist the temptation to use it as a substitute for a genuinely creative response to his material.

4 · Illustrators at work

**a symposium of illustrators' drawings
and an account by some of the
artists themselves of their chosen
methods of work**

It occurred to me that it would be useful to supplement my own extended account of the development of a line illustration by inviting a number of fellow artists to describe their own methods of work. No two illustrators tackle the job in exactly the same way, and the student should find, I believe, a fascinating variety of approaches for his consideration in the next few pages. I have done my best to bring together artists with widely varied styles so that their expertise may cover as much ground as possible.

Beneath their separate accounts of the way in which they carried out their specimen drawings, I have added a very short comment of my own. In this, I try to summarize my own professional reaction to the drawing, hoping thereby to 'nudge' the student just a little closer to the core of things.

The reader may find it rewarding to compare this body of work with that of the earlier masters of the art of illustration discussed in my first chapter. In spite of the enormous stylistic differences that will be immediately apparent, the clear-cut line of artistic descent is often equally evident.

All the work displayed in this chapter serves to remind us that illustration is something other than superlative drawing or a display of technical know-how. Unlike painting and sculpture, an illustration has a direct function, sometimes persuasive as in the case of an advertising drawing, sometimes falling into a literary or journalistic context. Illustration can never be a private exercise in graphic experiment unrelated to a specific purpose. Where it becomes this, it may be in itself enormously interesting but it will, by definition, no longer be illustration.

Edward Ardizzone

32

Edward Ardizzone was born in 1900. At 26 he quit the tedium of a city desk to attend life classes at the Westminster School of Art. He gave his first show of pictures in 1928 and his first illustrations, for *In a Glass Darkly*, appeared in 1929. He has since illustrated many books including his own *Tim* series. In 1940 he was appointed an Official War Artist.

Edward Ardizzone

EQUIPMENT Heavy Hot press paper; a hard pencil; a pen holding a nib called 'Mitchell's post office pen No. 0784', and any good indian ink.

METHOD I first make a fairly elaborate drawing in tone with my hard pencil. The point of using a hard pencil being that the resulting drawing is grey and will not get in the way of the ink drawing which follows.

Then using the back of my nib I make a fairly light and hesitant line round the main forms. This is like making a new drawing, as one does not exactly copy the pencil underneath but re-draws and extemporizes as one goes along.

The next stage is to block in all the main areas of shadow with an even horizontal hatch and rub out the underlying pencil. One then has a slight but complete little picture in light and shade.

The third stage is to elaborate the drawing, carrying it into the shadows, and to augment the shadows by cross-hatching.

Finally, by heavier cross-hatching particularly in foregrounds, one suggests the local colour, and by accenting the outlines here and there one gives an added sense of depth.

I always try to avoid finishing any one part of the drawing at the expense of the rest but try to build it up in stages, just as if one was painting a picture.

If I make a mistake I never use process white but scrape out the offending area with a knife and re-draw. Hence the necessity of using good paper. (Illustrations by courtesy of William Heinemann Ltd. and *The Listener*.)

The delicious world of Ardizzone has, to our delight, been with us for a long time now. His subtly unemphatic drawings invariably reflect a true illustrator's response to his material in their thoughtfulness and literary sensitivity. R.J.

Eric Fraser, FSIA, is a painter in oil and water-colours, pen and ink; he has exhibited in the Royal Academy and the S.S.A. His work has appeared in many magazines and books. He has also done mural paintings, in 1947 for the London Tea Centre, and for the Festival of Britain in 1951.

Eric Fraser

The illustration here reproduced is from 'The Tale of Hammād the Badawī' in Volume I of four volumes of *The Book of the Thousand Nights and One Night*, an exotic collection of tales of fantasy and imagination from the Middle East of many centuries ago.

Before starting to illustrate this I had to collect many examples of Persian manuscript paintings and architecture in order to present an appropriate feeling of period and place. Then, having read the story to be illustrated and got a mental image of an incident which seemed to offer possibilities of an exciting design, I did a small rough as a first visual. That this rough should be small I consider important, for it is thus easier to obtain a co-ordinated design. The eye can more easily assess the balance of masses, the continuity of line and the valuable repetition of shapes. Having achieved a satisfactory arrangement, I next drew the finished picture to approximately one and a half times reproduction size, in pencil on a suitable hard-pressed art board. Next, with a firm pen, such as Gillott 303 or Hinks Wells 303, and *waterproof* indian ink, all outlines were drawn in, and then the black areas filled in with a fairly fine sable brush. Finally, with a flexible fine pen and white poster colour thin enough to flow freely, all white lines were put in and edges cleaned up. Any necessary alterations were made by washing out the white, re-blacking with ink and re-drawing. The basic principle in this type of illustration is the play of movement between white areas broken by black lines and black areas by white. (Drawing from *The Book of the Thousand Nights and One Night*, published by The Folio Society for its members in 1959.)

Fraser's formidable talents as an illustrator are crowned by a powerful gift for graphic organization. In this department his mastery is complete. His dramatic handling of large areas of full black played off against the delicacy of his linear drawing is unique in contemporary illustration. R.J.

Eric Fraser

35

David Gentleman was born in 1930, studied at the Royal College of Art, lives in Camden Town and works in partnership with his wife doing freelance typography, display, press advertisements, book illustrations and wood-engravings, murals, fabrics and wallpapers; he usually spends two or three months each spring travelling in Calabria, Provence, Andalucia or Brittany, drawing and painting water-colours.

David Gentleman

I was asked to design two murals in laminated plastic for the saloon of a ship plying between Scotland and Northern Ireland. Their over-all shape was long and shallow, being 25 ft. × 3 ft., and both subject matter and style were left to my own choice.

I decided to suggest landscape themes taken from the wilder aspects of both countries, and to treat them in a free and evocative manner. As each mural would be made up of three equal panels, I first attempted six vignettes, but they looked too much like scaled-up book illustrations; so I finally resolved on a long unbroken design, taking care that the less complicated areas coincided with the joins in the plastic. On the opposite page is a 3 ft. wide section from the Irish mural.

I wanted to draw on a surface giving enough variation of texture to remain interesting when enlarged four times, so I chose blotting-paper and kept the drawing fairly loose, having first worked out the design very fully. The free nature of the composition allowed me to include objects for their own interest, regardless of place or scale, and the final size of details often bore little relation to reality – some, like the shells and

stones, appearing far larger than life-size. Certain passages were drawn in great detail while others were left relatively vague and unexplained.

Part of the material I found in books about each country – on traditional tools and utensils, such as the wooden pannikin in the illustration; and for the rest I used *objets trouvés* from beaches and fields, previous drawings and water-colours, and some photographs of my own of stone textures and plant forms.

Well known as an engraver-illustrator, Gentleman has chosen to discuss another of his activities. Notice how the freedom and 'attack' of his basic drawing is subtly complemented by the delicate hatching employed for textural and tonal areas.   R.J.

Paul Hogarth, FSIA, was born in 1917 in Westmorland. He trained as painter at Manchester College of Art, and in London at St Martin's School of Art. He has drawn in the Far East, Europe and Africa. His albums include *Defiant People* (1953), *Looking at China* (1955), *People Like Us* (1958), *Irish Sketchbook* (1962), and he contributes to foreign and British periodicals. Parallel to activities as artist-reporter is his work as book illustrator; he has illustrated Dickens for continental publishers, Conan Doyle and O. Henry for the Folio Society, and Olive Schreiner for Limited Editions Club of New York, and represented *British Book Illustration* Arts Council/ SIA in 1959/60. He lives and works in Suffolk.

Paul Hogarth

Drawing 'on-the-spot' is rather like being asked to plunge into a swimming pool in early spring. It requires an active identification with the everyday that no artist really feels inclined to give without effort. Often, the result will vary because there are days when one feels like communicating, and days when it would be impossible. Yet, as an end in itself, or as a means of making sketch-book studies, it is one of the most stimulating ways of working because it is unpredictable.

This drawing of a Belfast bar was done in about an hour. First I made rough notations for a composition exploiting signs and other features. Then I started drawing the interior with a conté chalk pencil, working directly on sheet paper clipped to a light-weight piece of hardboard. I like working on a good laid paper that will also take a wash. Using this type of paper ensures that the chalk strokes will be sufficiently dispersed, making a drawing of this kind more easily reproducible by the line process.

I kept an eye on the activity which began to unfold as the men came in for their midday pint. I needed a face, a personality expressive of the rich Edwardian flavour of the place. But persuading barman Tommy Kelly wasn't easy even with the help of a pint. He was afraid of being teased. Only after encouragement had been given by his customers did he relax enough to become a natural model. What had started out as an interior with figures had ended up as a setting for a portrait drawing. The original drawing was then immediately fixed with a mixture of synthetic alcohol and shellac flakes.

'Tommy Kelly, Barman at the *Bee*, Falls Road, Belfast' appeared in *Irish Sketchbook* and is reproduced by courtesy of the artist and the publishers, Messrs Hutchinson.
One's eye rests so happily on this shapely drawing that it may all too easily overlook the basic gravity of the artist's approach. Hogarth's brilliant graphic reportage is so balanced that our sympathies are engaged, first by the sinuous linear grace of his drawings and then by the warmth of his very human response to his subject. R.J.

Paul Hogarth

Dodie Masterman studied drawing and painting at the Slade for four years. Though illustrating furiously for private enjoyment from childhood onwards, it was not until an exhibition of her drawings brought invitations from publishers to work for them that she recognized the possibility of a career for herself in illustration.

Dodie Masterman

I never think about how I am going to use zip-a-tone tints until I have finished a drawing which makes sense without them. Then I like to freely dramatize with the tints, applying them like a wash, which adds some new function to the drawing with a character of its own, but which does not neutralize the feeling behind the part played by the pen.

In the case of my own sort of drawing, where forms are enclosed in an impulsive broken line, it rarely works to take the contour too literally; the tint must approximate to the meaning of the pen lines, but comment on this meaning in their own independent manner. Tints enable one to contrast areas of regular texture or pattern in a very evocative way. Some tints are comically apt for certain purposes and others achieve unexpected subtle effects. The drawing opposite has several tints on skirt and top; if I want a part to change for reasons of form or light I use any contrast which serves my purpose. I draw in varying ways to suit my reactions to places or period. This is never deliberate, it just happens. I have to identify with people or things to draw them. Only in this way can I find out how somebody would stand or look, to suggest a moment or mood suitable to the text. I don't visualize, I *feel* where a chair, a door, has to be in relation to a figure. (Illustration by courtesy of the artist.)

The use of adhesive tints as an adjunct to line-drawing lends itself to a great deal of abuse. The taste with which Mrs Masterman uses this hazardous medium serves to remind us that, in the right hands, all things are possible. R.J.

Dodie Masterman

41

Robert Micklewright

42

Robert Micklewright was born in 1923 in Stafford-shire, and studied drawing and painting at Wimbledon School of Art. During the war he spent five years in the infantry, Northumberland Fusiliers and Rifle Brigade, and served in North Africa, Italy and Greece. After the war he went to the Slade for three years and took a Diploma in Fine Art. He is now a freelance illustrator and Sunday painter.

Robert Micklewright

Illustration in the *Radio Times* for a television adaptation of Graham Greene's novel *The Power and the Glory*.

The problems involved in drawing for the *Radio Times* are not typical of illustration in general. The illustration is basically an advertisement for the programme that is to be transmitted – a book jacket rather than the illustration inside the book.

Television plays are particularly difficult to illustrate because the pictures the viewer will see on the screen are obviously not available at the time the drawing is being executed, and irritating discrepancies are difficult to avoid between the illustrator's conception and the actual set. The illustrator must therefore choose a scene that does not clash with the camera's view of the play. For example, when a character in the play opens a door on the set and walks out of camera range into the village square. Close-ups of the characters must be avoided for the same reason.

On the practical side, time is a serious problem. The illustration must be completed in three days, including the necessary preliminaries; reading the play, finding reference, working out the composition.

This illustration had to fit in with all these general requirements. Photographic reference of Mexico was necessary and was obtained from the public library, magazines and my own reference files. Then the composition was worked out on thin paper, bits constantly re-drawn by sticking fresh paper over the original composition with Cow gum, then transferred on to board by rubbing the back with a soft pencil and tracing over again, and finally drawn in with indian ink. This illustration was reproduced roughly 4 in. square. (Illustration by courtesy of the *Radio Times*.)

He has been called the illustrator's illustrator. In this subtly composed drawing, the artist points up the terrible vulnerability of his hunted priest by isolating him in the centre of the drawing and against the oddly ominous background of an utterly average small town. So carefully planned a drawing might easily have become laboured in the final stage but Micklewright's execution is everywhere crisp and lively.   R.J.

Ian Ribbons

Ian Ribbons, MSIA, ARCA, studied at Beckenham Art School and the Royal College of Art, with India and Burma and field-guns sandwiched in between. His main influence at college was the English comic tradition, though he now feels it is played out. Free-lances and teaches design at Guildford School of Art, but considers design inseparable from painting, and illustration from drawing. He thinks the main job of an illustration is to suggest all the things and space there is no room to describe.

Ian Ribbons

An unspecified number of drawings, unspecified size, on London night life for *Harper's Bazaar*. This drawing concerns late hours' drinking in a Smithfield pub. (Others ranged from night-clubs to tramps.)

A night's meander with notebook through London, including Smithfield. One always forgets details of clothes (the particular hang and creasing of a porter's smock, its exact length).

Begin next day. Slowly, roughing in pencil. I wanted to stress the intrusion on a worker's pub. Pencil scribbles of heavy porters staring solidly at pathetic figure in background. They become ever larger, more menacing, crowding out reveller. Reluctantly put him in foreground. Try him walking, staggering, leaning at angles, but looks vulgar. Finally, try him collapsed, but blissfully ignorant of downfall. Try several porters behind, plus detailed pub, but seems too complicated. Settle for one porter, hoping he'll suggest rest. Do fairly careful pencil drawing on detail paper. For placing and basic stance of figures. Play safe. Trace outlines, use pen on top. Looks stilted, pub too detailed, looks stuck on. Repeat; temper rises at second dud. Try again without tracing, drawing quickly, as if image is going to vanish at a moment's pause. In pen and unfixed ink. Seems almost O.K. but needs colour. Add black to hat with brush. Dislike reveller's head, looks ill rather than drunk. Look up John Leech to see how he did it. One or two experiments on odd paper. Acting session in front of mirror. (Someone passing in street stops in amazement.) Try about four or five more heads. One seems about right, is cut out, stuck over. (Illustration by courtesy of *Harper's Bazaar*.)

Ribbons's engaging account of the evolution of his drawing catches something of the *élan* of the drawing itself. But his spirited handling of his subject would not have been possible without the self-assurance engendered by the careful research he describes. R.J.

45

John Ward, ARA, FSIA, studied at Hereford School of Art and the Royal College of Art in the good bad old days. He worked for *Vogue* after leaving the Army, paints people and draws architecture. Loves working for other people.

John Ward

I like drawing women, architecture, plants, still-life, animals and children, and I like to be hurried gently by a loving publisher. I like to do a run of illustrations so that my eye and mind are filled with the subject.

I need a good female model who can act – I am bad at 'making things up'; I can use my model for all characters, male and female, except children, and since I have an abundance of these, there is no difficulty.

I never compose the illustration or plan it in any way, but draw directly in indian ink from the model and attempt to make the point of the drawing at once. This sometimes leads to the making of several versions; but if I use the steady, block-it-in-first method, the drawings begin to have a mean neatness and become full of tedious mannerisms.

I have always been very interested in the scribbles authors send to their illustrators – they so often are much more lucid and forceful (if crude) than the professional's effort. The letters of painters often contain perfect illustrations.

The decorative illustrator has done great harm to the job, and often far too much time is spent in thinking about the weight of illustration to type (typographers have become far too uppish) and not nearly enough to seeing that the lights in the eyes are reflecting the proper mood.

An illustration should be a diagram that makes a point as clearly as the word 'Gentlemen' does to a desperate man. Wood-engravings and wood-cuts I dislike, as I do illustrated books on thick paper – the 'fine edition' – unless they are of a botanical or scientific nature. (Illustration by courtesy of The Hogarth Press Ltd.)

Ward's light-hearted account of his approach to illustration should not be allowed to obscure his total sincerity. For him, spontaneity is all, and whatever hinders directness of attack is ruthlessly eliminated. Artists of this type must aim always to be in peak form, since for them there are no ready-made clichés to fall back on when invention flags. R.J.

John Ward

47

Brian Wildsmith

48

Brian Wildsmith was born in 1930 in Penistone, Yorkshire. From Barnsley School of Art he won a scholarship to the Slade, where he studied painting and drawing under Sir William Coldstream. He has illustrated twenty-three books, and paints when time allows.

Brian Wildsmith

The first task of the illustrator is to choose his subject. Knowing this he must then attempt a sharp, exciting translation of it which is not only complementary to the written word by which it is inspired but is also a thing of beauty in its own right. This is the ideal at which I aim and hope might some day achieve, for in the same way that a phrase of words or musical sounds can have an innate beauty regardless of what it is expressing, so the same principle can be applied to an illustration. The finished work is then exactly right for that particular medium. A drawing in pen and ink should not look as though it were first a pencil drawing afterwards inked over, but should have sprung, excitingly and spontaneously, almost of its own accord so that each line forms its counterpart quite naturally while being balanced against the preceding line.

This is the basis of my working rule. It has difficulties, but what drawing hasn't? It means keeping a razor-edge attitude; it means learning all about the subject to be drawn beforehand and then, while consciously forgetting but subconsciously remembering the construction and detail, throwing the image on to paper. It also means sometimes drawing the subject over and over again until the working rule is satisfied. The drawings shown were produced in this way. The horse and cart was a first drawing, while the one of Boris Godunov was drawn many times until the figures fell into place and the drawing made its own form, fitting the allotted area. (Illustrations by courtesy of The Oxford University Press and the Monotype Corporation Ltd.)

The vitality of Wildsmith's drawings is self-evident but, for me, they have an even rarer quality. Entirely satisfying though they are as black-and-white drawings, they seem to throb with colour. The coruscating textures in his Godunov drawing somehow suggest a Byzantine richness of golds, reds and purples. R.J.

49

Ronald Searle was born in 1920 in Cambridge. He has worked widely for British, American and continental magazines and illustrated a number of books, including recently three volumes of Dickens. He studied at the Cambridge School of Art and, after serving in the Army from 1939 to 1946, began freelancing as cartoonist and illustrator.

Ronald Searle

This drawing, 'The Old Bailey', was commissioned by the American magazine, *Holiday*, as a light-hearted illustration to a factual article on the Old Bailey. I was given complete freedom to fill one page in some way that would set the scene of a court in action, as photographs were not available. From the time of receiving the manuscript to the time of posting the finished drawing back to America, there were only three days available for the work. Under normal circumstances, it would have been necessary during this time to visit the Old Bailey and memorize the detail, as sketching in courts is illegal; but fortunately, all the background reference I needed was available from a previous commission, the fruits of three weeks of sitting-in on a murder trial, memorizing little details of the court-room each day and noting them down immediately after leaving the building.

This left me free to concentrate on some action which might give the reader a moment of amusement. After searching for an angle which would represent English law in action fairly clearly to a foreigner, I decided to draw the scene from the prisoner's point of view, from the Box. With the full artillery of a Criminal Court confronting a prisoner and the possibility of a monstrous crime on the calendar, the situation was made ludicrous by presenting the criminal as a self-possessed mouse, and at the same time emphasizing the rather Dickensian atmosphere of the scene.

This preliminary skirmishing was noted down very roughly in thumb-nail scribbles. Then, with the general idea of the composition of the drawing in mind, I scaled up the working area to about half up; this was less than usual as the page size, $12\frac{3}{4}$ in. $\times$ $13\frac{3}{4}$ in., was abnormally large. I then pencilled in the composition, starting with the architectural features and the furnishings of the court, which were, of necessity, factual.

Once the setting was complete, the action began to suggest itself, and it was a short move from the domination of the prosecution, waving an exaggerated weapon, to hit on the idea of an entirely horrified court facing an unconcerned accused.

50

Reprinted by special permission from
Holiday, copyright 1960, by The Curtis Publishing Co, USA

Ronald Searle

The preliminary pencil work was carried out in detail, working with a B pencil on fashion board with a cartridge surface. Once the idea was fully worked out, which took about three hours, the washes were laid in to emphasize the gloom of the scene, but kept well away from faces or essential fine lines that might be weakened by tone.

When the washes were dry, the pen work was added and worked as rapidly and as freely as possible over the pencil to capture a feeling of spontaneity in the line. Working with an ordinary fountain pen to cut out stopping and dipping, and using the back of the nib for the rougher outlines of the dominant figures, the drawing progressed downwards from the judge, to the prosecution, to the prisoner, and then worked round to the main body of figures in the court.

When the whole of the line had been laid in, the washes were strengthened, final touches added, and the odd unnecessary line scratched out with a razor blade. After the pencil work had been cleaned off, broken lines were checked for reproduction. The whole work took about six hours.

If, at this stage, the final drawing lacks the immediacy of the original thought, then (time allowing) I scrap the whole thing and use it as a guide for re-drawing. Fortunately, in this case it was unnecessary, but if I ever have the slightest uneasiness about the finished work, I re-draw it at once rather than attempt to scratch and patch. I feel it is essential for work of this nature to appear spontaneous. The moment an illustration appears laboured, it loses atmosphere, and with it – life.

A lively intelligence is at work in even the slightest of Searle's drawings. See how, in the above highly organized set piece, he so sites his wretched prisoner that one cannot but identify with him. Every line of the drawing crackles with vitality and its effect is the more hilarious when one recalls the ponderous gravity of the real thing.   R.J.

From *A Phoenix too Frequent* by Christopher Fry (O.U.P.)

And more beside

All of the artists whose work has appeared in the last pages are established figures with enviable reputations who need little introduction to the student of illustration. This is also the case with some, but not all, of those that follow. I have not attempted a comprehensive symposium of current illustrators but have tried rather to display the stylistic variety of contemporary work. The drawings are shown in no particular order and each is accompanied by a biographical note by the artist himself – or herself, as in the case of our first illustrator, an interesting American newcomer.

Colleen Browning is a young Irish-born painter who has made her home in America, where she exhibits regularly. She has shown in all major American annuals, and in such foreign exhibitions as the Spoleto Festival and the Inter-American Biennial in Mexico City. She has won awards at a variety of shows, including the Carnegie International and at Stanford University. Her work is in a number of American museums. (Illustration by courtesy of Doubleday Dolphin Book.)

Charles Keeping, MSIA, was born in Lambeth in 1924. He studied art at the Regent Street Polytechnic from 1946 to 1952. He has illustrated books for Oxford University Press, Bodley Head, Abelard-Schuman, the B.B.C. and many others. His lithographs have been exhibited in London, Italy, Australia and the U.S.A. He now teaches lithography at the Regent Street Polytechnic and drawing at the Croydon College of Art. (Illustration by courtesy of University of London Press.)

Cecil Keeling, born at Teddington in 1912, studied at Putney and Chelsea Schools of Art, while at the same time working for a printing firm; he has always concentrated solely on work for the printing press. Main interests apart from book and magazine illustration are wood engraving, typography and graphic design generally. Member of Society of Wood Engravers and Society of Industrial Artists. (Illustration by courtesy of *The Listener*.)

Don Higgins was born in Essex in 1928. He studied illustration and graphic design at Wimbledon School of Art and the Royal College of Art, and worked at the B.B.C. as a graphic designer, producing illustrations for music and drama programmes and filmed title sequences for drama serials. He has since combined book illustration with work as a television producer. (Illustration by courtesy of BBC Television.)

Jacob Landau was born in Philadelphia in 1917, and educated at the Philadelphia Museum College of Art, the New School, New York, and the Académie de la Grande Chaumière, Paris. He has had three one-man shows, and has exhibited extensively in Europe and the U.S.A. He is currently instructor in graphic design, Department of Graphic Arts and Illustration, Pratt University, New York. (Illustration by courtesy of the artist.)

Michael Ayrton was born in 1921. His activities include authorship, stage designing, painting and sculpture and, of course, the illustration of books. His work in this field includes drawings for *Poems of Death* in 1945, *Summer's Last Will and Testament* in 1946, *Macbeth* in 1951, and the *Human Age* in 1956. (Illustration by courtesy of Methuen Ltd.)

Mervyn Peake was born in Kuling, Central China, in 1911, and was educated at Tientsin Grammar and Eltham College Academy Schools. He has exhibited in London, New York and Dublin. He has illustrated many classics – *Alice in Wonderland*, *Treasure Island*, etc.; written and illustrated children's books – *Captain Slaughterboard Drops Anchor*, *Rhymes without Reason*, etc.; written three novels – *Titus Groan*, *Gormenghast*, *Titus Alone*; two books of poetry. He gained the Heinemann Award for Literature, and published in 1962 *The Rhyme of the Flying Bomb*, *A Ballad Poem with drawings*. (Illustration by courtesy of Chatto & Windus Ltd.)

Seong Moy studied at the St Paul School of Art, Hans Hofmann School of Art, and the Art Students League of New York. He has been awarded a John Hay Whitney Fellowship, a Guggenheim Fellowship, and prizes from the Chicago Art Institute, the Audubon Society, and many others. He is represented in the Metropolitan Museum, New York, the Whitney Museum, the Museum of Modern Art, New York, and others, and has exhibited at national and international exhibitions.

Milton Glaser was born in New York in 1929. Attended Cooper Union Art School and went with a Fulbright Scholarship to Bologna, where he studied etching with Giorgio Morandi. In 1954 he joined a number of other designers to form the celebrated Push Pin Studios. He teaches at the New York School of Visual Arts. (Illustration by courtesy of Leo Lionni, *Opera News*, USA.)

David Knight, MSIA, was born in 1923 in Surrey. He studied at the Wimbledon School of Art, and has freelanced since 1948. His first commissions were for the *Radio Times* and the early numbers of *Contact* magazine. Books: Gallico, *The Small Miracle* (Michael Joseph); the *Pepe* books for Faber and Faber; *Don Quixote* (Faber); Cecil Roberts, *Wide is the Horizon* (Hodder and Stoughton); Roger Pilkington's books in the *Small Boat* series (Macmillan); various school publications, including, for the last eight years, the BBC drawings in the *French for Schools* pamphlets. (Illustration by courtesy of the Monotype Corporation Ltd.)

62

James Boswell, a New Zealander, trained as a painter at the Royal College of Art in the 1920s. In the 1930s he began to make satirical drawings of the social scene; during army service he made realist, reportage drawings. He was Art Director of Shell Petroleum till 1947, and Art Editor of *Lilliput* magazine till 1951. Since then he has worked freelance, as designer, illustrator, journalist, and painter once again.

Terence Greer was born in Surrey in 1929 and had a normal middle-class-secondary-education up-bringing. The greatest impression visually remembered from childhood was the Hollywood films of the 1930s. He studied painting at Twickenham, St Martin's and the R.A. Schools. Consuming interests: jazz, the cinema, photography, the graphic work of Picasso, in fact, anything that looks and sounds stimulating. (Illustration by courtesy of the artist.)

64

Peter Reddick was born in 1924 in Essex. He studied at Cardiff School of Art, the Slade School of Fine Art and the London School of Printing and Graphic Arts. Member of the Society of Industrial Artists. Field of work: typographic and graphic design as a salaried designer and freelance. He lectured at Kwame Nkrumah University, Kumasi, Ghana, 1960–62. (Illustration by courtesy of Penguin Books Ltd.)

John O'Connor is a painter by first choice, who has for several years maintained a deep and absorbing interest in working with the printing industry. He has every respect for the high technical skill of the printer, but would like to see a broader use of graphic work in reproduction. He exhibits at the Zwemmer Gallery, and has paintings in a number of collections, public and private, in Britain. (Illustration from *The Saturday Book*, 1962, by courtesy of Hutchinson & Co.)

66

Sydney King was born in 1928, and trained at Manchester Regional College and the Ruskin School, Oxford. Later, at the Royal College of Art, he studied painting and stained glass. On leaving the College he became a graphic designer for A.R.T.V., and later graphic design editor for Shell Chemicals, with whom he is still associated as consultant. His first show of paintings was held in 1962. (Illustration by courtesy of Associated-Rediffusion Ltd.)

John Plant, ARCA, is 47 years of age. He spent seven years at the Sheffield School of Art studying drawing, painting, pictorial design, modelling and sculpture; and then four years at the Royal College of Art, specializing in mural decoration and graphic design. During the war he was an instrument repairer in the R.A.F. For five years he was a visiting instructor at Camberwell School of Art; and for fifteen years he has been an illustrator, etc., with an advertising agency. (Illustration by courtesy of the artist.)

68

Anthony Gross is 57 years old. He was born in London, and educated at Repton, Slade and Academie Julian. A painter and etcher, he exhibits with London Group, and extensively in Britain, France and the U.S.A. Animated cartoons for *La Joie de Vivre* 1934, *Foxhunt* 1937, *Round the World in 80 Days* 1939. He has illustrated many books, including the memorable *Forsyte Saga* for Heinemann. (Illustration by courtesy of William Heinemann Ltd.)

Pearl Falconer began her professional career in a commercial studio and studied in the evenings, first at St Martin's and then at the Central School of Arts and Crafts. Later she freelanced for the national dailies and magazines. She now works exclusively on book illustration and painting. (Illustration by courtesy of *The Listener*.)

Quentin Blake, MSIA, was born in 1932. He has had no formal art training, and read English at Downing College, Cambridge, before becoming a freelance illustrator. He has done many covers and other drawings for *Punch* and *The Spectator*. His other work includes book jackets and illustrations to children's books for Penguin Books, Faber & Faber, Hutchinson and other publishers. (Illustration by courtesy of the artist.)

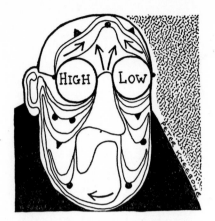

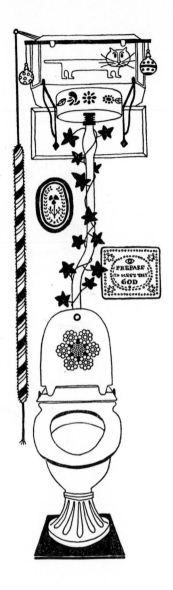

Peter Kneebone was born in 1923 in Yorkshire of Anglo-French parentage. M.A. Oxford; he did not attend art school. He worked on the Festival of Britain and as a television producer until 1953, then wholly as a freelance graphic designer and writer after the publication of his first book. He now does work for newspapers, advertising, books, magazines, television, films, exhibitions and textiles. (Illustration on the left by courtesy of the *Radio Times*, and on the right from *The Intelligent Woman's Guide to Good Taste*, by courtesy of MacGibbon & Kee Ltd.)

72

Michael ffolkes, MSIA, was born in 1925. Studied at St Martin's and Chelsea Schools of Art where he took painting. In 1946 his first drawings appeared in *Lilliput* and *Punch*. He later held one-man shows at the Leicester Galleries and the Arthur Jeffress Gallery. Has illustrated the *Daily Telegraph's* 'Way of the World' column for the last six years. (Illustration reproduced by permission of *Punch* and the Museum Press Ltd.)

Gerard Hoffnung. His tragically early death in 1959 robbed us of one of the gayest and most talented practitioners of the art of illustration. He was the creator of the hilarious Hoffnung Musical Festivals. Apart from his work for British and American magazines, he wrote and illustrated many books. (Illustration by courtesy of Dennis Dobson Ltd.)

Betty Swanwick, MSIA, trained at the Goldsmiths' College School of Art, Royal College of Art, and Central School of Art and Crafts. She has designed L.P.T.B. posters, Shell-Mex and other advertisements; written and illustrated three novels published by Poetry, London, Arthur Barker; illustrated children's books, Christmas cards, book jackets. She is a member of the Society of Mural Painters, and has done murals for the Festival of Britain 1951, Evelina Children's Hospital, etc. (Illustration by courtesy of the artist.)

Derrick Harris was a distinguished engraver-illustrator who died in 1960. His work appeared extensively in the *Radio Times*, and he illustrated a number of books including a memorable *Humphrey Clinker*, published by The Folio Society for its members in 1955, from which these are taken.

George Mackie was born in 1920. He has spent three years at Dundee College of Art, six years as pilot in Bomber and Transport Commands, R.A.F.; two years at Edinburgh College of Art after the war; six years freelancing in graphic design and part-time teaching; one year as salaried designer. Now he is Head of Department of Design in Gray's School of Art, Aberdeen. (Illustration by courtesy of the *Radio Times*.)

Gordon Ransom, ARCA, MSIA, was born in 1921 in Staffordshire. He trained at Woolwich School of Art and the Royal College of Art, and has been a freelance illustrator and designer since 1950. He taught at Winchester, Wimbledon and St Martin's Schools of Art, and has been Head of the Department of Graphic Design at St Martin's since 1960. He has exhibited at the Royal Academy and the New English Art Club. (Illustration by courtesy of Scottish Agricultural Industries.)

78

Joan Hassall, RE, FSIA, was born in 1906, the daughter of John Hassall, the poster artist. She studied painting at the Royal Academy Schools, and wood-engraving at Bolt Court School of photo-engraving and lithography. Her first commissioned work (1936) was *Devil's Dyke* by Christopher Hassall (Heinemann). Has illustrated books such as *Cranford, Sealskin Trousers* by Erik Linklater, *The Strange World of Nature* by Bernard Gooch, etc. In 1953 she designed the Queen's Invitation to the Coronation Ceremony. *The Wood Engravings of Joan Hassall* by Ruari McLean (O.U.P., 1960). (Illustrations by courtesy of Blackie & Son Ltd, Rupert Hart-Davis Ltd and the Saltire Society.)

Leonard Rosoman, ARA, FSIA, was born in 1913 in Hampstead, and studied
at King Edward VII School of Art, Durham University; the Royal Academy School,
London; and the Central School of Arts and Crafts, London. He has held one-man
shows at Roland Browse & Delbanco and the St George's Gallery, and has exhibited
at the Leicester Gallery, Leger Gallery, Edinburgh, Norwich, Dublin and New York.
His works have been purchased by the Arts Council, British Council, York Art
Gallery, Carlisle Art Gallery, Norwich Museum, Contemporary Art Society, and the
Victoria and Albert Museum. During the war he was official War Artist to the
Admiralty. He has had work published by the Oxford University Press, the Folio
Society, Hutchinson, Longmans Green, Collins, Hogarth Press, Cresset Press,
Penguin Books, Weidenfeld and Nicolson, and Max Parrish. He is now tutor at the
Royal College of Art. (Illustration by courtesy of The Oxford University Press.)

Faith Jacques, MSIA, studied at Leicester College of Art from 1940 to 1942, and finished her training at the Central School of Art from 1946 to 1948. She taught (part-time) at Guildford School of Art 1949–51. Her practical work has been mainly in the field of magazine and book illustration, and she has contributed to *Lilliput*, *Strand*, *Radio Times*, the *Listener*, *House and Garden*, etc. She has also illustrated several children's books, the *Saturday Book*, etc., and designed three commemorative postage stamps in 1960 and 1961. She is now teaching part-time at Hornsey College of Art. (Illustration by courtesy of Unilever Ltd.)

Anthony Gilbert, MSIA, was born in 1916, and studied at the Goldsmiths'
College of Art. Illustrations for *Vogue, Lilliput, Radio Times, Strand,* etc. Murals for
Festival of Britain 1951. Stained glass work. Drawing in permanent collection of the
Victoria and Albert Museum. He works for an advertising agency. (Illustration by
courtesy of *Lilliput*, Hulton Press Ltd.)

82

Leonard Weisgard was born in 1916 in New Haven, Connecticut, U.S.A. He has more than 200 illustrated books to his credit, and holds American Institute of Graphic Art awards, Art Directors' and Society of Illustrators' awards, and a Caldecott Medal. His books have had international publication, and he has exhibited in museums throughout the United States and Europe. (Illustration from Grimm's Fairy Tales, by courtesy of Nelson Doubleday.)

John Minton, who died in 1958, was a painter-illustrator of great distinction. As a teacher at both the Camberwell Art School and the Royal College of Art, he had a profound influence. He had exhibited many times since the end of the war, and his enormous corpus of illustrative work includes drawings for *Treasure Island*, *Le Grand Meaulnes* and *Time Was Away*, as well as most of the quality illustrated magazines. (Illustrations by courtesy of the *Radio Times*.)

Heather Standring was born in 1928 near Bristol. She studied at the Central School of Arts and Crafts under Meninsky. After a variety of jobs both in Britain and abroad, she began freelance practice and has made many drawings for British and American publishers of books, magazines and newspapers. (Illustration by courtesy of Anthony Blond Ltd.)

Edward Bawden has illustrated a number of books, including *The Arabs* for Penguin Books, *The Histories of Herodotus* and *Salammbô* for the Limited Editions Club of New York, and *English as She is Spoke* for the Lion & Unicorn Press of the Royal College of Art, London.

Edward Bawden by J. M. Richards (Penguin Modern Painters), *Edward Bawden* by R. Harling (English Masters of Black and White). (Illustrations by courtesy of Limited Editions Club of New York.)

Brian Robb, painter and illustrator, was born in 1913 at Scarborough, and studied at Chelsea and the Slade. He used to work for *Punch* and *Night and Day*, and did publicity work for Shell and Guinness. After the war he concentrated on book illustration proper, but now devotes most of his time to painting. He is a member of the London Group and teaches at the Royal College of Art and at Chelsea. He lives in Hampstead. In 1962 he held a one-man exhibition of his paintings at the Arthur Jeffress Gallery. His books include *My Middle East Campaigns, The Golden Asse, Twelve Adventures of the Celebrated Baron Munchausen* and *Æsop's Fables*.

87

Fritz Wegner, MSIA, was born in Vienna in 1924 and came to England in 1938.
He studied at St Martin's School of Art. Since 1946 he has worked as freelance
artist for English and American publishers, book and magazine illustrations and a
variety of advertising and design. He is a visiting teacher at St Martin's, is married
with three children, and lives in London. (Illustration by courtesy of Blackie & Son
Ltd.)

88

C. Walter Hodges, FSIA, studied at the Goldsmiths' College. His first published drawing was in the *Radio Times* in 1931. Since then he has illustrated over sixty books, and written four. He served in army camouflage in the Second World War. He has designed for stage, films and exhibitions, and painted murals, and is an authority on the Elizabethan theatre. Married, two children. Bites his nails and has an old tom cat. (Illustration from *Red Indian Folk and Fairy Tales*, by courtesy of The Oxford University Press.)

Susan Einzig. Her studies at the Central School of Arts and Crafts 1939–42, were followed by a war-time factory stint. In 1946 she taught with John Minton and Keith Vaughan at the Camberwell Art School. Her recent work includes drawings for *Tom's Midnight Garden* (Oxford University Press), and *The Children's Song Book* (Bodley Head). (Illustrations by courtesy of The Oxford University Press.)

S. R. Badmin, RE, RWS, ARCA, FSIA, was born in 1906 in Sydenham. His publications include *Village and Town, Trees in Britain,* and *Farm Crops in Britain.* He has illustrated *British Countryside in Colour, Trees for Town and Country, Famous Trees,* and the *Shell Guide to Trees and Shrubs.* (Illustration by courtesy of the *Sunday Times Publications Ltd.*)

Leonard Baskin, sculptor and wood-engraver, was born in New Brunswick in New Jersey, U.S.A. in 1922. The son of a New York rabbi, he attended New York University School of Fine Arts from 1941 to 1943, and Grande Chaumière, Paris, in 1951. He has been associate Professor at Smith College, Northampton, Mass., since 1953. (Illustration by courtesy of the artist.)

Barbara Jones, ARCA, FSIA, was born in Croydon, and trained at the Royal College of Art. The books she has illustrated include *The Isle of Wight* (King Penguin) 1950, *The Unsophisticated Arts* 1951, *Follies and Grottoes* 1953. She has also painted murals for the Festival of Britain in 1951, for S.S. *Orcades* (1948–49), S.S. *Oronsay* (1952), S.S. *Orsova* (1954), S.S. *Oriana* (1960), etc.; and has exhibited at the White-chapel Art Gallery ('Black Eyes and Lemonade') and at the Tea Centre ('Royal Occasions'). (Illustration by courtesy of Darton, Longman & Todd.)

Lynton Lamb was born in 1907. He is a member of the London Group, and on the staff of the Slade School. Books: *Preparation for Painting* and *Drawing for Illustration*. He has served on the Arts Council and the Council of Industrial Design; past President, Society of Industrial Artists. He designed the binding of the Bible used at the Coronation, and high-value postage stamps of the new reign. (Illustration by courtesy of Faber & Faber Ltd.)

Maurice Wilson was born in 1914 in North London, and attended Hastings School of Art and the Royal Academy Schools. He writes: 'Much of my work concerns animals but I do not regard them as a special subject but, like ourselves, part of the whole scene, as it were. I also do a lot of Palaeontological work!' (Illustration by courtesy of the artist.)

Laurence Scarfe, ARCA, FSIA, member of the Society of Mural Painters, has been a lecturer at the Central School of Arts and Crafts since 1944. He has illustrated many books since 1938, and was Art Editor of the *Saturday Book*. He did murals for the Festival of Britain 1951, and for S.S. *Orcades*. Publications: *Rome, Fragments in the Sun* 1950. (Illustration by courtesy of Shell-Mex and B.P. Ltd.)

Stefan Martin at 26 is a well-established wood-engraver, with steady commissions from publishers. His works can be seen in an English publication, *Motif IV*. He apprenticed at the Sander Wood Engraving Company in Chicago, while studying painting at the Art Institute of Chicago. He was recently awarded the Louis Comfort Tiffany Foundation grant in the field of graphic arts. He resides and has his studio in Roosevelt, New Jersey. (Illustration for *Natural-History* Magazine, November 1960).

Trevor Willoughby was born in 1926 at Hull, Yorkshire. He started his career in the Merchant Navy, but left it in 1947. He attended night school at the Hull College of Art in 1949, and in 1952 took an advertising job in London. He studied at night school at the London School of Printing and Graphic Arts, under John Ward, and has been freelancing since 1954, drawing for the *Queen, Homes and Gardens*, and advertising. Method of working: draws direct from the model. (Illustration by courtesy of the Prudential Assurance Co Ltd and Pritchard Wood & Partners Ltd.)

John Sewell was born in 1926. He studied at Hornsey Art School 1948–51, and at the Royal College of Art 1951–54. After a period of freelance graphic design, he became Head of Graphic Design for B.B.C. Television in 1955. Resumed freelance practice in 1957 and holds several design consultancies. (Illustration by courtesy of *Town*.)

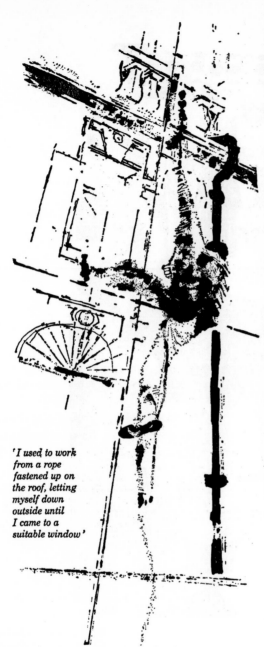

'I used to work from a rope fastened up on the roof, letting myself down outside until I came to a suitable window'

was tremendously proud of the school and the achievements of his pupils, and he was always telling us we were as good as every other boy in any school.

The first thing I did when I got there was leave, but, as the place was right out in the middle of nowhere in the country, I didn't get far before I was caught. Wathen had me up in front of him. He didn't get angry, just pointed out I was silly and would have to be moved to a Borstal if I didn't behave, and they were dreadful places which I wouldn't be happy at. He gave me a few swishes with his cane, nothing serious, and left it at that: he didn't hold it against me, neither then nor any other time when I did anything wrong.

I wasn't all that far from being happy at Carlton. I enjoyed the joinery, and I read a lot. Their own library wasn't up to much, but I arranged with other boys to bring me back books from the public library in the town, so I didn't do so badly. It was there I first came across Oscar Wilde—"The Ballad of Reading Gaol," naturally—but that led me on to his other works, and I still rate him the tops. I went through most of Dickens, and a lot of Somerset Maugham. "Cakes and Ale" I didn't take to, but "Liza of Lambeth" and "Alien Corn" were terrific, particularly "Liza," which I've re-read several times since.

CALL-UP PAPERS

I discovered Upton Sinclair, Theodore Dreiser, Scott Fitzgerald, George Orwell. "Seven Pillars of Wisdom" I thought a fantastically good book, but the other Lawrence, D. H., never appealed : I thought he was a creep. I liked some of Hemingway, but when I found out he enjoyed bull-fighting I went off him. One time I gave myself about fifteen headaches trying to get through James Joyce's " Ulysses," but I just wasn't up to it intellectually, although I'm always kidding myself that some day I'm going to try again. I liked a few poets, too : Auden, Robert Graves, William Plomer, and, of course, Dylan Thomas. But I can't " get " poetry unless I read it aloud, and I'm too embarrassed to do this in front of anyone else. I even liked Kipling, but only for the jingle, not the jingoism.

Then I got my call-up papers for the Army.

To say I wasn't a big success in the Army wouldn't be true : I wasn't any kind of success at all. Over things like regulations and discipline, our points of view were diametrically opposite. The Army's all right for wooden-heads who like playing soldiers—but for wooden-heads who don't, like me, it's a waste of time; particularly theirs.

MORE TROUBLE

I was put in the Service Corps, which was terrible, and after a while I went absent. After a few days in Norwich the Redcaps nicked me, and I ended up in Colchester glasshouse, doing a spell of refined Army punishment like running on the spot, in the full of heat of August, in full service marching order : buttoned-up overcoats, helmets, packs, rifles, the lot. I don't know what this is supposed to do for you except fill you with black hatred for the bastards who put you through it.

I got in more trouble as soon as I was back with the unit. They were

Anthony William Colbert, MSIA, was born in 1934, and spent his childhood in Littlehampton, Sussex. Scholarship to Worthing Art College in 1949. He managed to combine National Service and Farnham Art School for eighteen months; then commercial studios in Brighton and London, and then spells of farm work in Sussex while compiling folio as credentials for more fulfilling work. Engaged, upon presenting it to *The Observer*, in 1959. Hobbies: Working, looking and listening to music. (Illustration by courtesy of *The Observer*.)

5 · The painful realities

a guide for the would-be illustrator
to the practical handling of his
business affairs and other matters

Profit and loss

One of the hazards that the freelance artist must constantly face is the period of time that so often passes before he is paid for his work. He will find that, although many of his clients will present no difficulties in this direction, others may keep him waiting possibly three to four months before settling his account. This makes it imperative that he keeps a careful eye on his day-to-day expenditure. To keep abreast of this situation he would do well to record in a simple account book the day he delivered each job and the agreed fee, so that he can readily check his current position at the bank against the outstanding credit represented by work still unpaid for. A carefully kept record of this type may do much to mollify querulous bank managers who are able, with its help, to assess the artist's real credit position.

Invoices

It is customary with commercial clients to render them what is called an invoice, on which is set out a statement of the work completed and the agreed fee for it. It may be that the artist will have received from the client a written order for the job which will probably carry a job number. This number facilitates the codification and costing of work and should appear on the artist's invoice. Over the page will be found a simple form of invoice which shows the way in which they are normally composed.

Income tax and the illustrator

The haphazard nature of freelance work is hardly conducive to orderly book-keeping, but with a little planning on the lines suggested above, the artist's business affairs need not become too irretrievably muddled. In this connection, he would do well to

I N V O I C E

Rudolf Lovell, 117, Grosvenor Court, London W.1

18th January, 1963

To Peabody Publicity Ltd.,
    5 Macadam Square, W.C.2.

                    Job Number XYZ 122/73

Client - Glumm Rubber Corp.Ltd.

To preparing roughs and finished
drawings for the following subjects-

1	Child with beach-ball	£26	5	0
2	Children with canoe	£47	5	0
		£73	10	0

consult an accountant through whom his income tax dealings could be conducted. His accountant will almost certainly advise him to keep all his bills, particularly those directly relevant to expenses incurred in conducting his freelance practice. The bills may later need to be produced to substantiate the artist's claims for allowances should the Inland Revenue Inspector query them.

Beneath is set out a list of items of allowable expenditure, but special circumstances may often justify further claims whose validity should be discussed with one's accountant.

Rent of studio

Full cost if the artist works in quarters apart from his residence or a proportion of his rent if he works at home.

Artist's materials

All are claimable.

Use of a car

A proportion of the cost of running and maintaining his car is claimable if it is used in pursuance of his professional employment.

Telephone charges

If the artist works at home, a percentage of his calls is allowable. If he rents a separate studio his calls are all allowable, subject to agreement by the Revenue Officer.

Reference books

Here the position is not entirely clear-cut, but a generous allowance is normally made.

Postage

Difficult to keep details of expenditure. It is worthwhile to arrive at an average figure by watching expenditure carefully for a period of, say, two months.

Entertainment

Costs incurred in the entertainment of clients and prospective clients are deductible, but material evidence in the form of bills may well be demanded and, even then, disallowed. This is a matter for reasonable adjustment between the Revenue Officer and the artist's accountant.

Travelling

Journeys incurred in visits to clients, agents and to places of research are all claimable.

Professional expenses

Subscriptions to professional societies are allowed.

Work charges

Special type-setting and photography connected with the illustrator's work are allowed – but once again, keep your bills.

Stationery (including printing)

Allowable.

Cost of accountant

Allowable.

Life Insurance premiums

Allowable.

Agents

A profound and illuminating book may some day be written about the relationship between artist and entrepreneur, the creative element and the commercial. Actors, authors and artists all have recourse to agents whose job it is to promote and market the talents of their clients.

The initial role of the artist's agent is to introduce the illustrator's work to all potential users of it. Then, on the offer of a commission, he forms the link between client and artist, carefully conveying the problem and instructions from one to the other. The work done, he then carefully checks it to see that it has been properly carried out and delivers it to the client. For these services his rate of commission is likely to be 20 per cent to 25 per cent of the total fee agreed between himself and the client. Whether or not to use an agent must be a question for the individual artist. Circumstances may themselves make an agent well nigh imperative for certain artists. For country-based illustrators their usefulness is immediately apparent, and artists of a nervous or retiring disposition find them invaluable.

I myself believe recourse to an agent to be a wise step for the beginner, who rarely knows the market as well as the experienced professional. Once established, the artist may feel himself adequate to deal with the client directly and indeed, may come to value the more direct contact. On the other hand, he may feel content to leave the liaison work in the practised hands of his agent, winning himself thereby more working time at the drawing-board.

To their surprise, many beginners experience difficulty in persuading agents to take them on. There are usually quite straightforward reasons for this. All too often the artist is not yet ready to launch himself on the market and his work may still show evidence of his inexperience and lack of skill. Naturally enough, few agents care to waste their time pressing immature work on reluctant clients. Then again, the agent may already represent an artist whose work is very similar in kind to that of the newcomer. Agents usually feel happiest with as varied a team as possible. In this case, an approach by the artist to another agent is called for. If his work has real merit, he should experience no difficulty in finding one. In this connection, a section of the *Writers and Artists Year Book* contains the names and addresses of thirty-eight artists' agents. Most of them indicate the type of work handled by them.

The package

It may be that some comments on the attitude of the illustrator to the presentation of his work will prove helpful. Basically, as long as the illustration 'works', is reproducible and satisfies both artist and client, that is an end to the matter. On the other hand, by 'packaging' the drawing attractively, by cleaning and mounting it carefully and giving it a protective overlay, the artist does two things. He has taken the trouble to safe-guard his work from possible damage and he has obliquely made the point that he considers it well worth taking pains over! In a package-conscious society, those who seem to care nothing for the presentation of their 'product' may be thought to take little or no pride in it. They must not then be surprised when what seems to be their own negative valuation of their work comes to be accepted by their clients.

Standards

The actor who regularly fails to appear for performances is very quickly castigated by his professional colleagues and his future engagements are likely to be few indeed. Similarly, illustrators who win themselves reputations for unreliability are almost always by-passed in favour of more conscientious artists. The vagaries of the artistic temperament are unendearing to art editors and production managers with pressing dead-lines to meet.

Roughs

In certain circumstances, an illustrator's clients may ask him to submit roughs. These may vary, depending on the nature of the job, from the merest pencil scribble to work with a degree of polish barely distinguishable from a finished drawing. The rough, no matter how summarily carried out, should be considered as seriously as finished work, since on its effectiveness may depend later gainful employment for the artist. It should be executed and presented with care and charged for independently of the final drawing which may or may not develop from it. It is difficult to suggest any clear-cut figures for rough fees, since these naturally vary with the nature and com-plexity of the job. A useful general assessment might be 20 per cent of what the artist would expect to charge for a finished drawing of the same subject. In passing, fees for roughs as well as for general graphic work in the illustration field are dealt with in two leaflets compiled by the Society of Industrial Artists. These are called 'Terms of agreement and schedule of average fees for Book Illustration', SIA 260 and 'Schedule of Average fees for Commercial Designs', SIA 142. These cost 1s. to non-members of the Society.

Finding work

C'est le premier pas qui coûte. Yes, but how to take it, where to begin? There is no royal road to success in illustration, no ordered progression that ensures acceptance. Some artists, it is true, seem to leap blithely over the wall at the first bound, but for most it is a long, hard climb. In an earlier section I considered the usefulness of the agent to the artist. Where the artist is lucky enough to have a good agent he may make real progress very quickly and his work will have been widely disseminated among all its potential users. Those, however, who prefer to face alone the cut and thrust of the market must make a careful study of it. Time should certainly not be wasted showing work in the wrong places. A comprehensive survey of the illustrator's market can be found in the invaluable *Writers and Artists Year Book*, which contains a section in which are listed some hundreds of publishers of books, magazines and journals. Many of these set out the sort of work in which they are interested and sometimes give some guidance as to the fees paid for freelance work. I myself believe that for the absolute beginner a little intelligent anticipation is called for and that, having familiarized himself with the scope of the market, he should prepare specimens of work with certain specific clients in mind. This serves to orientate his work in a concrete direction and allows prospective clients to gauge the realism of his approach.

Friendly advice can sometimes be sought from art editors and production managers who are normally kindly though busy people. Their views are likely to be clear-cut and realistic and the aspirant-illustrator would do well to ponder their findings. A sensible plan of action for the future might be laid down by a consideration of the advice gathered from, say, three or four separate opinions of the artist's prospects. In this way, the possibly idiosyncratic viewpoint of one professional may be balanced by the concensus of opinion represented by the others.

6 · The future for illustration

some thoughts on the prospect for illustrators and the new forms of graphic design in which they are playing a part

Nothing is more conducive to *angst*, self-searching and a sense of remoteness from life than the nature of the illustrator's work, the prolonged scratching away in isolation at his drawing-board. I am sometimes surprised that more of us don't opt out, take up market-gardening or something really forward-looking like market-research.

But take another look at the sixty or so drawings that form the fourth chapter, and read again the comments of the artists on their work. You will find there a quite extraordinary freshness and vitality. Surely, one feels, we should be in another 'golden age' of illustration with our artists as fully employed as were those of the 'sixties in the last century. But for all but the very few, the illustrators pickings do not amount to much and he is usually obliged to supplement his income by other means, usually teaching. 'Even when', as Lynton Lamb pointed out, 'he is successful, he will be entered too often. He knows that he will have to run while the going is good and, unless he is being paid royalties, will have little to show at the end of the season.'

Of course, books were never the only source of employment for black-and-white artists. In the pages of a host of weekly and monthly magazines employment was given to successive generations of our best illustrators, and in the United States the formidable talents of Winslow Homer, Arthur Boyd-Houghton, Remington and John Sloan enriched the remarkable 'pictorials' of their period. In Europe, Daumier, Delacroix, Lautrec and Steinlen had all made drawings for magazines and posters, and other artists of quality were not slow to follow where they led. In particular, the political convulsions which followed the First World War brought into being a remarkable group of satirical illustrators, deeply critical of the moral and social disintegration of post-war Europe. Their virtually total disenchantment, however, did nothing to diminish the vitality of their work and, distant though that immediate post-war period now seems, the powerful drawings of Beckmann, Otto Dix and George Grosz continue to excite us.

New directions

Biting social comment in graphic form is very little in evidence today since the conditions that provoked it no longer exist, at least in Europe and the United States. Commoner now is the use of artist-reporters by private and state-owned industries to celebrate their productive processes and the workers engaged in them. Ben Shahn, Hans Erni, Paul Hogarth and Ronald Searle are among the artists who have been intelligently employed in this way and, with the growth of self-awareness and concern for their public images, the great corporations are likely to increase opportunities for illustrators in this field. The house magazine, too, a relatively recent development brought about by industry's need to project to its employees a warmer, less remote *persona*, also provides work for the artist. In Britain, these new sources of employment to some extent eased the situation brought about by the death of three quality pictorial magazines *The Strand, Lilliput* and *The Leader* in which a number of English artists first established their reputations.

Magazines

Recently, a new crop of 'glossies', some of them old campaigners in new armour, has found new though largely decorative uses for illustrators. *The Queen, McCalls, Town, Esquire, Holiday*, all designed with a subtle art-editorial eye for photographic and typographic experiment, offer a whole range of new visual experience and delight in their eclectic wide-angled-lens view of modern living. Cars, letter-forms, bosoms, graffiti, all are grist to this euphonic mill, and among them the illustrator is carefully insinuated. How satisfyingly John Alcorn's or Milton Glaser's drawings are made to complement the superb photographs. It is surely a world of enchantment for the decorative illustrator, an apolitical Madison Avenue slanted Hall of Confectionery, heady with possibility.

Graphic design — perspectives

In conclusion, I feel we should briefly examine some of the newer designs fields in which illustrators have found a place or in which their services may be increasingly sought. These new developments, some of which are still in a semi-experimental stage, reflect a mid-century awareness of the value of visual symbols as opposed to purely literary ones. In the swift moving media of film and television it is sometimes possible to make a point more forcefully, poignantly or universally with a single graphic image. It is in providing such images that the new designer-illustrator can be of enormous value. His terms of reference are, of course, different from those of the book illustrator since he deals in a nimble-footed way with day-to-day ephemera and his effects do not endure to be pondered over. But this transitoriness is, let us face it, very much of our time, and there are certain gifted artists particularly well equipped to respond to it.

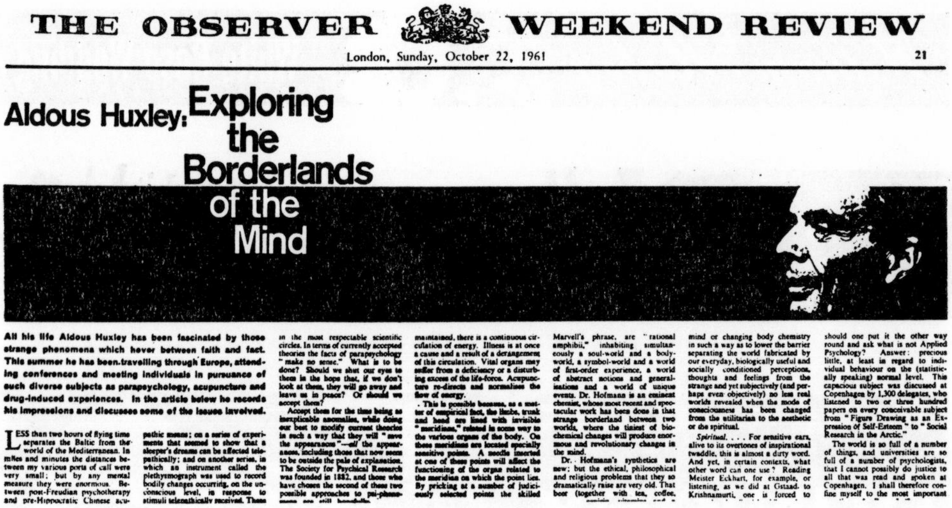

THE OBSERVER WEEKEND REVIEW

London, Sunday, October 22, 1961 21

Aldous Huxley: Exploring the Borderlands of the Mind

All his life Aldous Huxley has been fascinated by those strange phenomena which hover between faith and fact. This summer he has been travelling through Europe, attending conferences and meeting individuals in pursuance of such diverse subjects as parapsychology, acupuncture and drug-induced experiences. In the article below he records his impressions and discusses some of the issues involved.

LESS than two hours of flying time separates the Baltic from the world of the Mediterranean. In miles and minutes the distances between my various ports of call were very small; but by any mental measure they were enormous. Between post-Freudian psychotherapy and pre-Hippocratic Chinese acupathic means; on a series of experiments that seemed to show that a sleeper's dreams can be affected telepathically; and on another series, in which an instrument called the plethysmograph was used to record bodily changes occurring, on the unconscious level, in response to stimuli telepathically received. These

in the most respectable scientific circles. In terms of currently accepted theories the facts of parapsychology "make no sense." What is to be done? Should we shut our eyes to them in the hope that, if we don't look at them, they will go away and leave us in peace? Or should we accept them?

Accept them for the time being as inexplicable anomalies, while doing our best to modify current theories in such a way that they will "save the appearances"—*all* the appearances, including those that now seem to be outside the pale of explanation. The Society for Psychical Research was founded in 1882, and those who have chosen the second of these two possible approaches to psi-pheno-

maintained, there is a continuous circulation of energy. Illness is at once a cause and a result of a derangement of this circulation. Vital organs may suffer from a deficiency or a disturbing excess of the life-force. Acupuncture re-directs and normalises the flow of energy.

. This is possible because, as a matter of empirical fact, the limbs, trunk and head are lined with invisible "meridians," related in some way to the various organs of the body. On these meridians are located specially sensitive points. A needle inserted at one of these points will affect the functioning of the organ related to the meridian on which the point lies. By pricking at a number of judiciously selected points the skilled

Marvell's phrase, are "rational amphibii," inhabiting simultaneously a soul-world and a body-world, a symbol-world and a world of first-order experience, a world of abstract notions and generalisations and a world of unique events. Dr. Hofmann is an eminent chemist, whose most recent and spectacular work has been done in that strange borderland between two worlds, where the tiniest of biochemical changes will produce enormous and revolutionary changes in the mind.

Dr. Hofmann's synthetics are new; but the ethical, philosophical and religious problems that they so dramatically raise are very old. That beer (together with tea, coffee,

mind or changing body chemistry in such a way as to lower the barrier separating the world fabricated by our everyday, biologically useful and socially conditioned perceptions, thoughts and feelings from the strange and yet subjectively (and perhaps even objectively) no less real worlds revealed when the mode of consciousness has been changed from the utilitarian to the aesthetic or the spiritual.

Spiritual. . . . For sensitive ears, alive to its overtones of inspirational twaddle, this is almost a dirty word. And yet, in certain contexts, what other word can one use? Reading Meister Eckhart, for example, or listening, as we did at Gstaad, to Krishnamurti, one is forced to

should one put it the other way round and ask what is not Applied Psychology? Answer: precious little, at least in regard to individual behaviour on the (statistically speaking) normal level. This capacious subject was discussed at Copenhagen by 1,300 delegates, who listened to two or three hundred papers on every conceivable subject from "Figure Drawing as an Expression of Self-Esteem" to "Social Research in the Arctic."

The world is so full of a number of things, and universities are so full of a number of psychologists, that I cannot possibly do justice to all that was read and spoken at Copenhagen. I shall therefore confine myself to the most important

Design by John Marshall. By courtesy of *The Observer*

The general press

Our national papers are, with one exception, not remarkable for the distinction of their appearance, but there are departments in which some of them have broken into very promising new territory. The first of these is in the field of feature display, normally an embarrassingly tasteless mess, but in the hands of, for example, *The Observer* and the *Daily Express*, a very potent new design form.

Few would claim any very marked graphic merit for our British strip-cartoonists. Certainly none of them has the sheer virtuosity of America's Milton Caniff or Herge, the creator of Tintin. There is, however, one extremely gifted artist at work for the *Daily Mail*, Wally Fawkes, whose *Flook* strip has been consistently brilliantly drawn for fifteen years. His incisive line and unfailing wit have weathered a decade of deadlines and a multiplicity of script-writers and still show no signs of flagging.

FLOOK -- *Herren of Harlech* **by Trog**

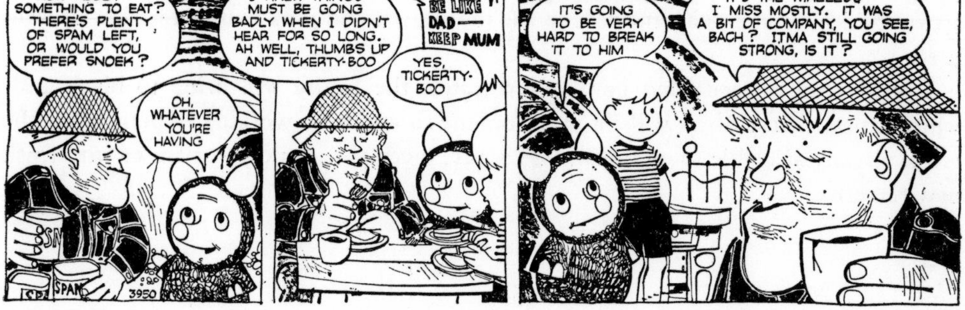

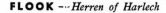

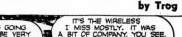

Reproduced by kind permission of the *Daily Mail*

Graphics by Ray Hawkey.   By courtesy of the *Daily Express*

Films and television

To date, the illustrator's work in films has been limited to one or two experiments, interesting in themselves but seeming to lead nowhere. Some years ago, a short was made in which drawings by John Minton, Ronald Searle and a small group of artists were set to words and music. Earlier, an animated cartoon film, *The Foxhunt*, with drawings by Anthony Gross was shown and enthusiastically received. But the film business in this country seems, in general, to have found little use for illustrators. From time to time, the credit titles of a British comedy may be embellished by a few amusing drawings but this is as far as things have gone. Television, on the other hand, has been considerably more adventurous. Extremely able illustrators are at work in this field and are imaginatively employed in a number of different ways. Educational programmes in particular are well served by artists and one sees an expanding future here. Television advertisers, too, may well come to see how valuable a fresh use of artists could become as an antidote to the indifferent and rank bad material at present used.

Nobody can foresee what new opportunities the future will bring to black-and-white artists. Most of us will be well content to continue working hopefully on the levels already available to us and will be ready, given the chance, to push on into fresh new territory.

Index